MIND BENDERS
GAMES OF CHANCE

IVAN MOSCOVICH

PENGUIN BOOKS

Penguin Books Ltd, Harmondsworth, Middlesex, England
Viking Penguin Inc., 40 West 23rd Street, New York, New York
10010, U.S.A.
Penguin Books Australia Ltd, Ringwood, Victoria, Australia
Penguin Books Canada Ltd, 2801 John Street, Markham, Ontario,
Canada L3R 1B4
Penguin Books (N.Z.) Ltd, 182-190 Wairau Road, Auckland 10
New Zealand

First published by Penguin Books 1986
Original concepts copyright © Ivan Moscovich 1986
This edition copyright © Eddison/Sadd Editions Limited 1986
All rights reserved

An Eddison · Sadd Edition
Edited, designed and produced by
Eddison/Sadd Editions Limited
2 Kendall Place, London W1H 3AH

Phototypeset by Bookworm Typesetting, Manchester, England
Origination by Columbia Offset, Singapore
Printed and bound in Hong Kong by Mandarin Offset
Marketing (H.K.) Limited

The design on the front cover contains a visual puzzle.
What do these three-dimensional shapes carved from
cubes like blocks of stone represent?

CONTENTS

INTRODUCTION

I have always been fascinated by puzzles and games for the mind. I enjoy brain games of all types – and like particularly those with some special aspect or feature. Those I like best are not in fact always the hardest: sometimes a puzzle that is quite easy to solve has an elegance or a 'meaning' behind it that makes it especially satisfying. I have tried to provide a good selection in this book: some are easy and some are fiendishly difficult but they are all tremendous FUN! Above all, I have tried to provide something for everyone, in order to share my delight in such puzzles and games as widely as possible.

Solving puzzles is as much to do with the way you think about them as with natural ability or any impersonal measure of intelligence. Most people really should be able to solve nearly all the puzzles in this book, although of course some will seem easier than others. All it takes is a common-sense, practical approach, with a bit of logic and – occasionally – a little persistence or a flash of insight.

Thinking is what it's all about: comprehension is at least as important as visual perception or mathematical knowledge. After all, it is our different *ways* of thinking that set us apart as individuals and make each of us unique.

Although some of us feel we are better at solving problems mathematically, and others prefer to tackle problems involving similarities and dissimilarities, and others again simply proceed by trial-and-error persistence, we all have a very good chance of solving a broad selection of puzzles, as I'm sure you will find as you tackle those in this book.

From long and happy experience, however, I can tell you one secret, one golden rule: when you look at a puzzle, no matter how puzzling it seems, simply BELIEVE YOU CAN DO IT, and sure enough, you will!

Lars Lidscori

HOW TO SOLVE PROBLEMS

To start things going, let's look at the different approaches that can be useful in solving puzzles.

First, the logical approach. Logic is always valuable, as it helps you work things out sequentially, using information received to progress step by step to the answer. This is especially true in games of *Chance*, which tend to be oriented toward mathematics and concentrate on using numbers for simple calculations, or on ordering arrangements of objects or figures. Examples of this can be found in the games *Magic Numbers.*

In problem solving, there may also be a need for an 'indirect' approach, whereby you arrive at an answer by perceiving and thinking about a subject in a way you have never done before. This depends on how you think normally, of course, and so for some people it may be helpful for certain puzzles, and for others for different ones. The first part of *Match Blocks* is solved most simply, quickly, easily and 'elegantly' using an 'indirect' approach of this kind.

The visual approach is also important, especially in this book because all the puzzles are presented in visual terms and require initial visual comprehension (or conceptualization) to be combined with understanding the text of the problem. This is particularly the case with the tricky puzzle set as *The 18-point Problem.*

In general, the puzzles in this book of games of *Chance* are of four types. They are concerned with:
1. simple calculation using patterns, objects or symbols;
2. spotting serial links and connections;
3. the laws of chance and probability – particularly in assessing the odds for or against specific events or results occurring;
4. ordering, combining or grouping objects or figures, following a defined rule, to achieve a stated target.

Examples of all four types are given on the following pages, together with the answers. See if you can solve them first without looking at the answers – then go on to enjoy the rest of the book! If you have any queries about any of the puzzles, or you would just like to get in touch, please write to me care of the publishers. I shall be pleased to hear from you.

SAMPLE GAMES

GAME 1

The Magic Square is possibly the oldest mathematical puzzle in existence. Examples have been found dating back to before 2000 BC. By AD 900 one Arab treatise was recommending that pregnant women should wear a charm marked with a Magic Square for a favorable birth.

Can you distribute the numbers 1 through 16 in this 4 x 4 square so that lines across, lines down, and major diagonals all add up to the same total?

Hint: Make each line add to 34.

GAME 2

Many IQ tests feature puzzles that initiate a series and then require you to carry on when they leave off. This means that you have to spot the links or connections between the figures or symbols that make up the series.

What is the next entry in each of these series?

a) A B D E G H J ....?

b) 36 28 21 15 10 6 ......?

c) • | △ □ ⬠ ......?

a) K
The series is alphabetical omitting every third letter.

b) 3
A series of subtractions: between each successive number, one less is subtracted each time.

c) ⬡
The number of sides in each figure increases by one.

There are quite a few possible arrangements for these numbers: for example, if you reverse the rows horizontally or vertically the answer is the same. This answer therefore is just one of many.

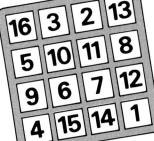

16	3	2	13
5	10	11	8
9	6	7	12
4	15	14	1

GAME 3

Two coins fall through the air, turning as they drop. Each coin has the usual two sides: heads (h) and tails (t). In how many combinations of those sides can they end up when they come to rest on a flat surface?

Well, one way of looking at the possible results is:

    heads heads
    heads tails
    tails tails

– three possibilities, from an overall point of view. Does that mean that there is a 1:3 chance of any one result?

Suppose we number our coins, odd numbers on the heads side, and evens on the tails. How does this help to prove that the odds of heads tails occurring is actually 2:4 or 1:2?

Numbering the two sides of the coins helps to show that there are, in fact, 4 possible results:

    heads(1) heads(2)
    tails(1) tails(2)
    heads(1) tails(2)
    heads(2) tails(1)

Consequently there is twice the probability of heads + tails occurring (2:4 = 1:2) as of either of the other two combinations (both 1:4).

GAME 4

In a darkened room there is a box of mixed gloves: 5 black pairs, 4 red pairs, and 2 white pairs. You find the box by feeling for it. How many gloves must you take out – without being able to see them – to make sure you have two of the same color?

And how many must you take out to make sure you have both the left and right hand of the same color?

To be certain you have 2 gloves of the same color you must take out 4 gloves – one more than the number of different colors.

To be certain you have a matched pair – both left and right hand of the same color – you must take out 12 gloves: one more than the total number of gloves for one or other hand.

(Solutions page 50)

MATCH BLOCKS

The blocks in columns on these two pages can be arranged in a 7 × 7 square formation so that the horizontal rows are numbered in succession from top to bottom 1 through 7, as shown in the diagram below.

The columns of blocks shown below and right can be used in two puzzles. You can make your own columns of blocks if you like, but a pencil and some thought with the grid should suffice.

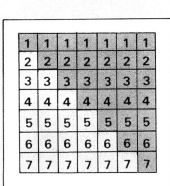

GAME 1

8

GAME 1

Rearrange the columns so that no number appears more than once in any horizontal or vertical row. (This should not take long.)

GAME 2

Arrange the columns again so that no number appears more than once not only in a horizontal or vertical row but also in a large or small diagonal.

GAME 2

(Solutions page 50)

FINDING THE KEY

Most of us carry a few keys around with us; some, like me, carry vast collections weighing down their pockets. It's not surprising, really, in view of the number of different things we now need to keep locked: automobiles, suitcases and briefcases, office doors and safes, even desks and bureaus at home . . . So here are a couple of puzzles on the subject – I hope you'll find the key to solving them.

KEYS TO THE KEYS

On a circular key ring there are 10 keys, all with round handles, in a specific order that you have memorized. Each fits one of 10 different locks. The trouble is, it's pitch dark: you can't see the key ring, you can only feel the keys with your fingers. If you had some way of telling in the dark which key was which, it wouldn't take you long to find any particular one you wanted. So you decide to give some keys different-shaped tops – but do you need 10 different tops?

What is the least number of different key tops you'll need to be sure, once you've felt them, that you've identified where you are on the ring? And would you put all the new keys together or give them some sort of arrangement?

Hint *Any symmetrical number or arrangement of keys will not help: you will still not know which way round you are holding the key ring. Use a pencil to mark the different shapes of key top to work out the solution.*

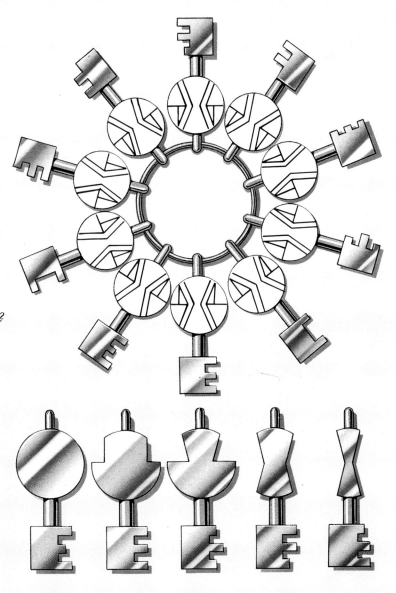

COMBINATION LOCK

A safe has ten locks in combination, requiring ten keys, each of which bears a letter inscribed on its handle. But to confuse thieves some of the letters are the same.

The safe opens only when all the keys have been inserted in the locks, the handles then spelling out a secret code word.

Fortunately, you have a diagram of the interior of the locks, showing the shapes of the appropriate keys. Otherwise you might have to spend a lot of time trying out all the possible 3.6 million combinations of ten locks. And of course you also know the secret code word . . .

What is the secret code word?

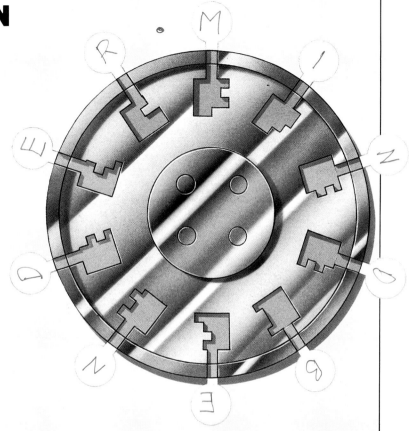

CONTINUOUS PATHS

Fifteen lines join the six points, or nodes, of a regular hexagon. Where each line crosses another there is a further node, giving a total of 19 nodes in all. Every line also carries an arrow: no matter where the arrow is located on this line, it makes the *whole* line directional.

The object of the game is to try to find a continuous path connecting all 19 nodes, starting anywhere (which becomes node number 1). You must always travel down lines – or parts of lines – in the direction of the arrow, and you may visit each node only once.

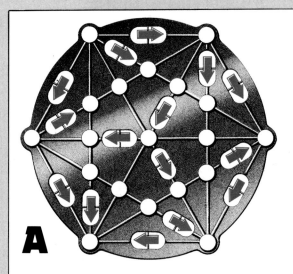

A

SAMPLE GAME

The sample game shown below proves that it is not so easy: an unlucky or unskilful player may reach a node from which he or she is then unable to move farther because the arrows are contrary. Yet it may be that only a single move – but a wrong one – has foxed the player.

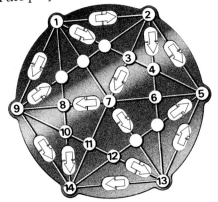

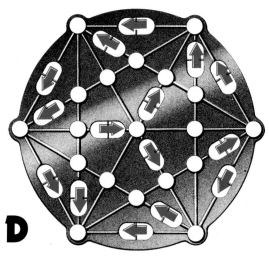

D

The first hexagon A (above) has arrows that point in the same directions as on the sample game. Can you complete the puzzle? Is there more than one node you can start from?

The other hexagons, B, C, D in this and the next columns have arrows arranged differently. Can you successfully find your way around all 19 nodes in each of them? Game B can end at only one node: which one, and why is this?

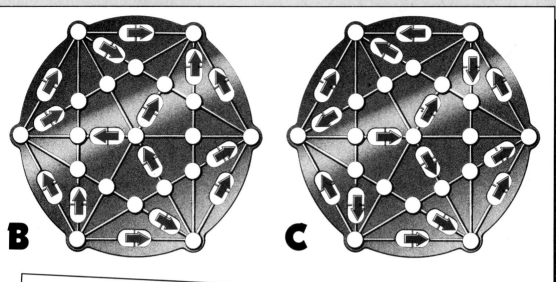

B

C

DEVISE YOUR OWN

Arrows should point in only one direction. In the hexagons below (E and F), however, all the arrows are two-headed, because I'm giving you a chance – *before* you start playing – to make up your own mind which direction you want the arrows to point. Shade off lightly in pencil the unwanted end of each arrow. Then play the game as usual.

This version of the game can also be played by two people, each taking turns to shade an arrow (until there are no more arrows) and make a move; the last to move is the winner.

The decision about which way each arrow points can also be determined by chance: toss a coin for each arrow – heads points left, tails points right.

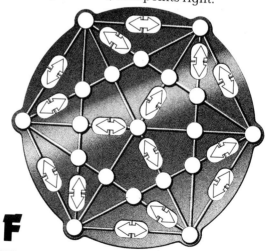

E

F

13

(Solutions page 52)

SLIDING COINS

In these games I challenge you to reverse the positions of sets of coins within a confined space. Cash-flow problems, you might say! If you can't find coins of the right size, counters will do. Small circles in the game bases show the centers of the possible positions of coins or counters; the miniature diagrams indicate the starting positions for

the games. One move involves moving a piece from its position to a free space; this need not be an adjacent space, but it must be reached without any other piece being disturbed.

Hint All three games can be played more easily if you construct (out of card, perhaps) bases of the shapes shown, in and on which your coins can slide. Solving the problems mentally is a more interesting challenge, however.

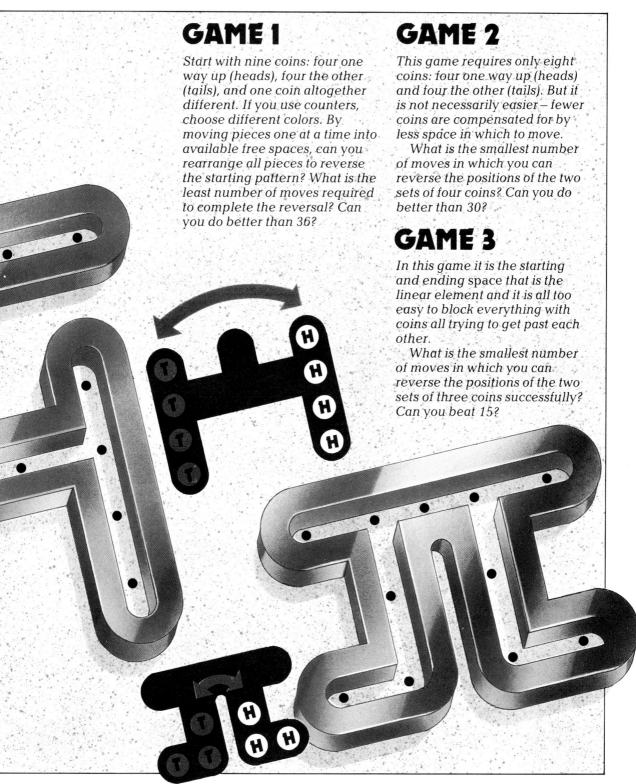

GAME 1

Start with nine coins: four one way up (heads), four the other (tails), and one coin altogether different. If you use counters, choose different colors. By moving pieces one at a time into available free spaces, can you rearrange all pieces to reverse the starting pattern? What is the least number of moves required to complete the reversal? Can you do better than 36?

GAME 2

This game requires only eight coins: four one way up (heads) and four the other (tails). But it is not necessarily easier – fewer coins are compensated for by less space in which to move.

What is the smallest number of moves in which you can reverse the positions of the two sets of four coins? Can you do better than 30?

GAME 3

In this game it is the starting and ending space that is the linear element and it is all too easy to block everything with coins all trying to get past each other.

What is the smallest number of moves in which you can reverse the positions of the two sets of three coins successfully? Can you beat 15?

15

MAGIC NUMBERS

'Magic Squares' – in which lines of numbers add up to the same total whether read horizontally or vertically, or sometimes even diagonally – have been the delight of magicians (and mathematicians) throughout history. Yet many other shapes can be used equally well, if not better. Some are actually simpler – like the Magic Cross. In most puzzles on these two pages, I have given you the total all the lines should add up to – the 'magic number'. With or without the magic number, can you fill in the required spaces in each line?

THE MAGIC WHEEL

In the Magic Wheel, can you distribute the numbers 1 through 9 around the nodes so that lines across the Wheel – from outer node to the center node and on to the opposite outer node – all add to the total 15?

THE MAGIC CROSS

The Magic Cross is only part of a Magic Square. Can you insert the numbers 1 through 12 in the squares so that lines across and lines down all add to the total 26?

SIX-POINT STAR

Magic Stars are based upon hexagons, heptagons and octagons. In the six-point Star, can you distribute the numbers 1 through 12 around the nodes so that each of the six lines adds up to the 'magic number', 26?

MAGIC NO 26

16

THE MAGIC HEXAGON

In the Magic Hexagon, can you distribute the numbers 1 through 13 around the nodes so that lines – from outer node to the center node and on to the opposite outer node, and also along each side – total 21?
Hint Look for the key center number.

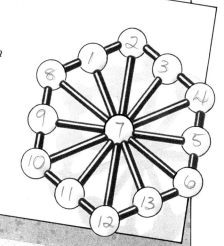

SEVEN-POINT STAR

In the seven-point Star, can you distribute the numbers 1 through 14 around the nodes so that each of the seven lines adds up to the same total? No magic number is given.
Hint Find a relationship between the highest number inserted in the six-point Star and its 'magic number', and you may be able to calculate the 'magic number' for the seven-point Star.

MAGIC NO

MAGIC NO

EIGHT-POINT STAR

In the eight-point Star, can you distribute the numbers 1 through 16 around the nodes so that each of the eight lines adds up to the same total? Again, no 'magic number' is given (but see the Hint above).

(Solutions page 54)

MAGIC NUMBERS 2

These Magic Squares are all slightly more complex than the other magic shapes in the book, even though they *are* merely squares. That is because either there is more than just addition to have to worry about, or there is some other restriction or condition affecting your choice that I have put in to perplex you.

In this 4 × 4 Magic Square can you distribute the numbers

1 2 3 4 5 6 7 8
−1 −2 −3 −4 −5 −6 −7 −8

so that lines across, lines down and the 2 main diagonals all total zero?

Now let's add a zero to the numbers to be distributed:

8 7 6 5 4 3 2 1
0 −1 −2 −3 −4 −5 −6 −7

This time all the lines actually do add up to a positive number. Which number?

Continuing this theme, can you distribute the numbers

12 11 10 9 8 7 6 5
 4 3 2 1 0 −1 −2 −3

so that lines across, lines down and the 2 main diagonals all total the same?

18

Now let's turn to a 3 × 3 Magic Square. First, can you distribute the numbers 1 through 9 in such a way that by subtracting the central number in any line of three from the sum of the outer two, all total the same, whether horizontally, vertically or diagonally?

Second, can you distribute the numbers
   1 2 3 4 6 9 12 18 36
in such a way that all lines across, lines down and diagonals when multiplied internally total the same number?

Third, can you distribute those identical numbers
   1 2 3 4 6 9 12 18 36
in such a way that, by dividing the central number in any line of three into the product (after multiplication) of the outer two, the lines all total the same horizontally, vertically and diagonally?

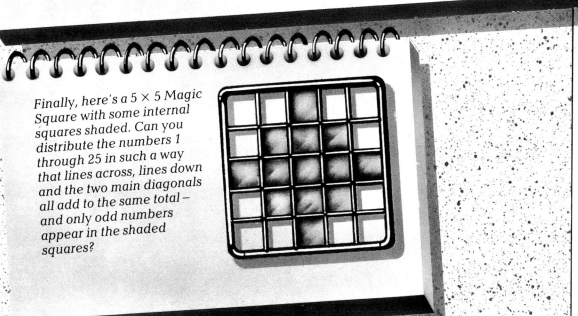

Finally, here's a 5 × 5 Magic Square with some internal squares shaded. Can you distribute the numbers 1 through 25 in such a way that lines across, lines down and the two main diagonals all add to the same total – and only odd numbers appear in the shaded squares?

(Solutions page 54)

COMBI-CARDS

Combi-cards are a bit like families: every member is quite individual, yet each one has some feature that is strongly reminiscent of another - so that in each, some of the others are combined.

In these three Combi-cards (below), each card has two numbers, one of which appears on one of the other cards, and the other on the other. (The set thus has a total of three numbers, each featured twice.)

SAMPLE GAME

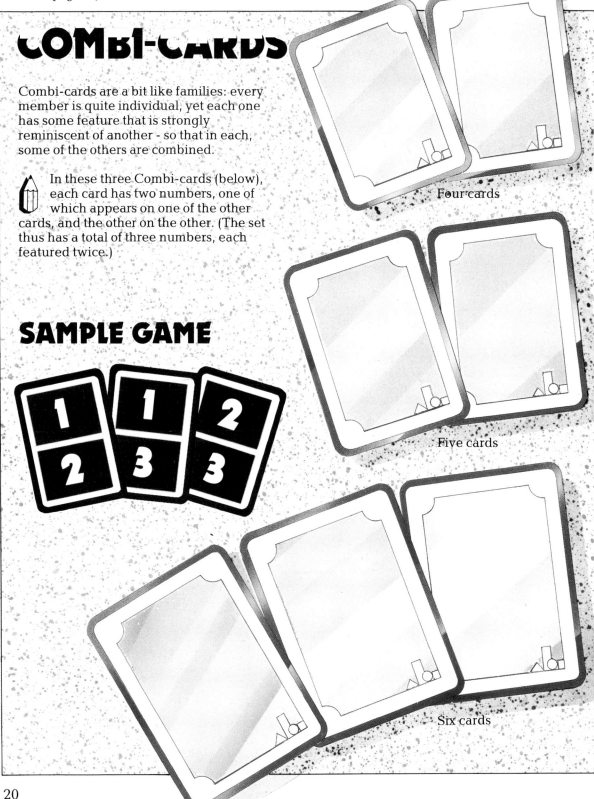

Four cards

Five cards

Six cards

20

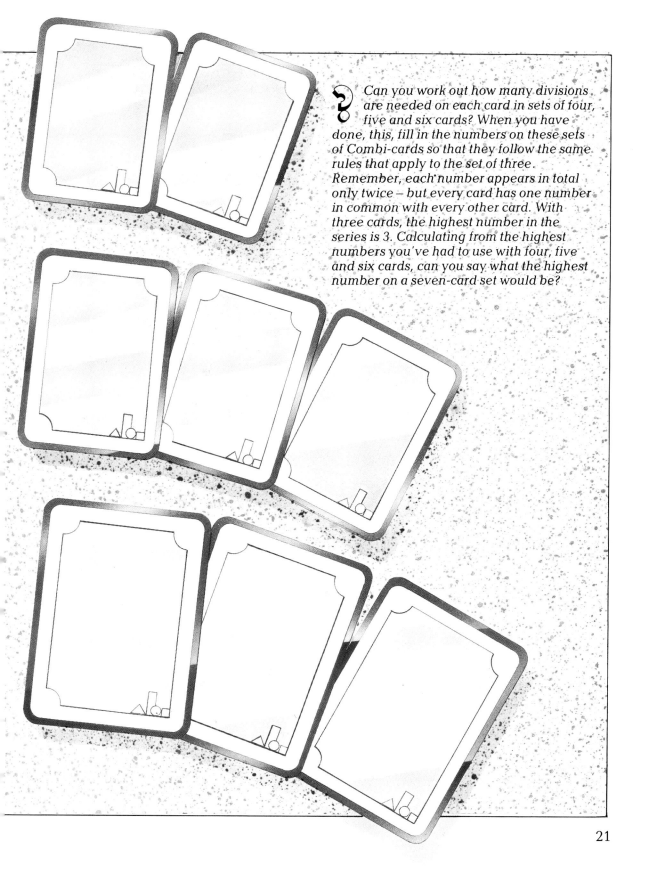

Can you work out how many divisions are needed on each card in sets of four, five and six cards? When you have done, this, fill in the numbers on these sets of Combi-cards so that they follow the same rules that apply to the set of three. Remember, each number appears in total only twice – but every card has one number in common with every other card. With three cards, the highest number in the series is 3. Calculating from the highest numbers you've had to use with four, five and six cards, can you say what the highest number on a seven-card set would be?

(Solutions page 55)

MONEY PROBLEMS

I find playing with money is always a chancy thing, even if you are only using coins as counters, as in the puzzles on these two pages. The first game involves rearrangement. The second and third are like board games, with a difference . . .

A RING OF COINS

Arrange 6 coins as shown: one is trapped in the middle of what is nearly a complete ring of coins. How can you slide the coins, one at a time, so as to get the trapped one out to the edge, and so complete the ring? Here's the catch: each coin moved must end up touching two others, and no other coins may be disturbed. But you can take as many moves to do this as you like!

Hint Coins not being moved may be left touching only one other coin.

SOLITAIRE

Place nine coins on the top board, leaving any one space free. Coins are removed by being jumped by another coin – every time one coin jumps its neighbor to land in an empty space, the jumped coin is removed; if the jumping coin can then jump a second or even a third coin, this is still part of the same move.

How many moves must you make to leave only one coin? Can you do it in fewer than six moves?

Now try the game with 14 coins on the lower board: leave space 4 free. In my best sequence I cleared the board of all but my jumping coin in nine moves – how about you? Why is it a good idea to start from space 4? Can you start from any other space and still clear the board successfully?

There are in fact only two other spaces to start from . . . which ones?

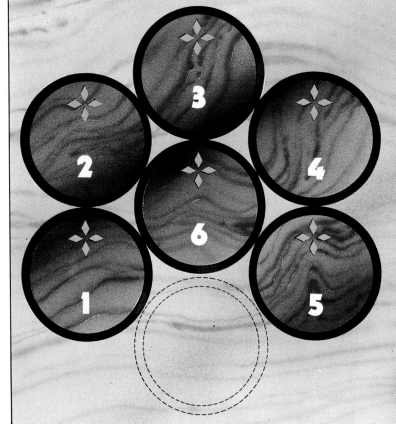

(Solutions page 56)

THE 18-POINT PROBLEM

This problem is all about locating fixed points in spaces that change dimension. Imagine you have a long strip of land in which there is a tree. Dividing the land into two halves, you plant another tree in the second half. Then you decide to divide your land again, and plant another tree. And again. And again. Each time, the trees already planted turn out, luckily, to be in their own separate plots.

Can you be foresighted – and farsighted – enough to plant your trees where they will be by themselves no matter how often you divide your land into equal parts?

The strip of land is represented here by a line, and the trees as dots or points.

THINK AHEAD

To give you some ideas about the methods – and the traps – in doing the puzzle, below we show an attempt that ended in failure at the fifth level: points 2 and 4 are in the same new area. Can you complete the 11-line grid farther below, following the principles outlined, so that on the eleventh level all 11 points (or trees) added serially are separately in their own plots?

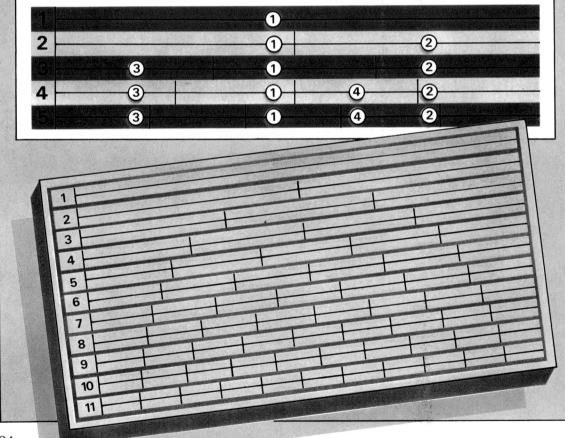

24

THE OPEN-ENDED CHALLENGE

You might imagine that with sufficient foresight the number of possible plots and trees within them (following the principles outlined) ought to approach the infinite. That is actually not the case: the limiting factors are the serial nature of the way points are added, and the permanence of the points once sited. But it is quite possible to successfully break the eleventh division-barrier – although again, once more to emphasize foresight, the strategy to achieve 11 divisions may be totally different from one to make (say) 17.

How far can you get?

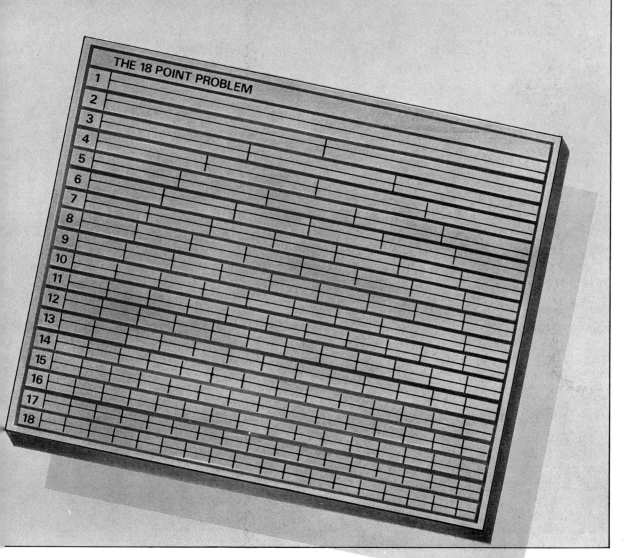

(Solutions page 56)

JUMPING COINS

For this game you need two sets of small coins, or counters in contrasting colors. With coins, use one set showing heads, the other showing tails. The object of the puzzle is to reverse the pattern by exchanging the positions of the two sets of coins or counters. There are four rules you have to observe:

- Only one coin can be moved at a time.
- A coin can move into an adjacent empty space.
- A coin can jump over one *of the opposite type* into a space immediately beyond it.
- A coin may *not* jump over another of its own type.

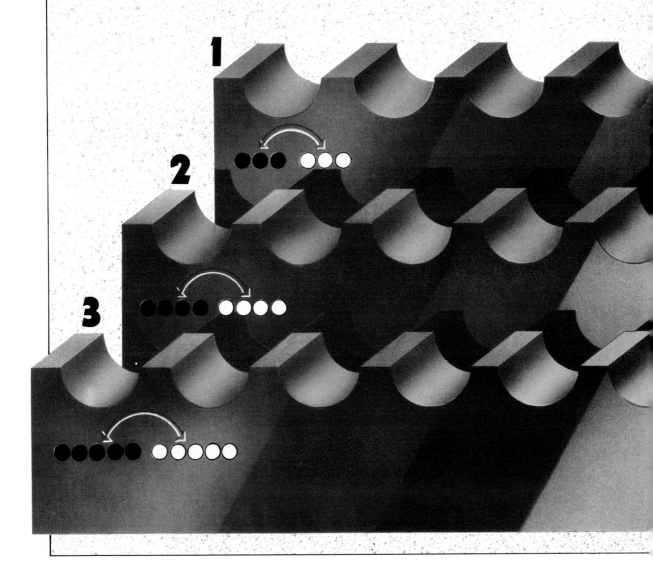

What is the minimum number of moves required to reverse the pattern with:

    a) four coins, two of each type? This game is shown (right): Answer, eight moves.

    b) six coins, three of each type? (See the board plan.)

    c) eight coins, four of each type?

    d) ten coins, five of each type?

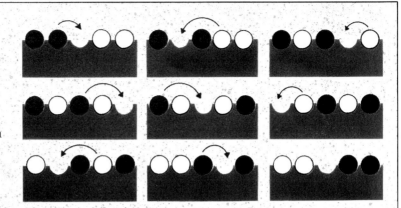

Can you spot a mathematical link between the first three solutions (to a, b and c) that will give you the fourth solution (to d) without your having to go through all the moves?

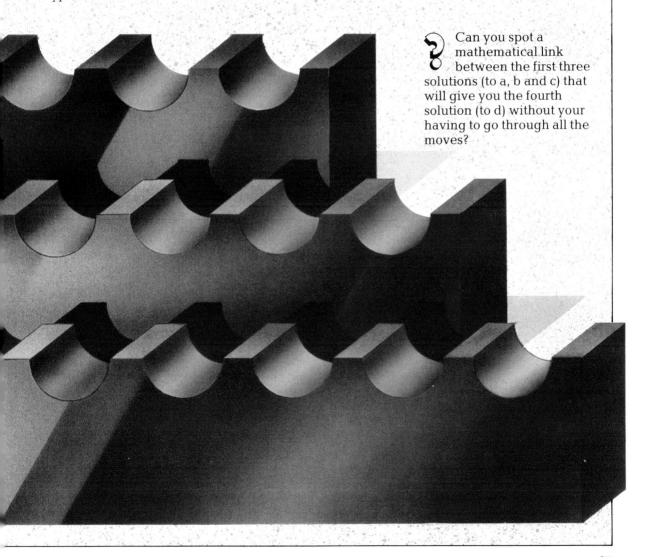

(Solutions page 57)

LIFE OR DEATH

Have you ever been in a situation where you have had to appear impartial when making a choice from a number of people? I have, and I know that, human nature being what it is, it's sometimes very difficult to suppress the urge to fix the odds for or against specific choices.

Elimination games depend on an apparently regular, and therefore impartial, selection that nevertheless realizes the desired (and distinctly partial) result. The games shown here are examples.

OUTER RING

Would you like to be Emperor of Ancient Rome? I'm sure you would. The only problem is that there are 39 of your friends and acquaintances who would like to be Emperor too. Can you think of a 'fair' and 'democratic' way to eliminate all the competition so that only you and one other candidate (an obvious no-hoper) are left – at which time you can ensure all those eliminated vote for you?

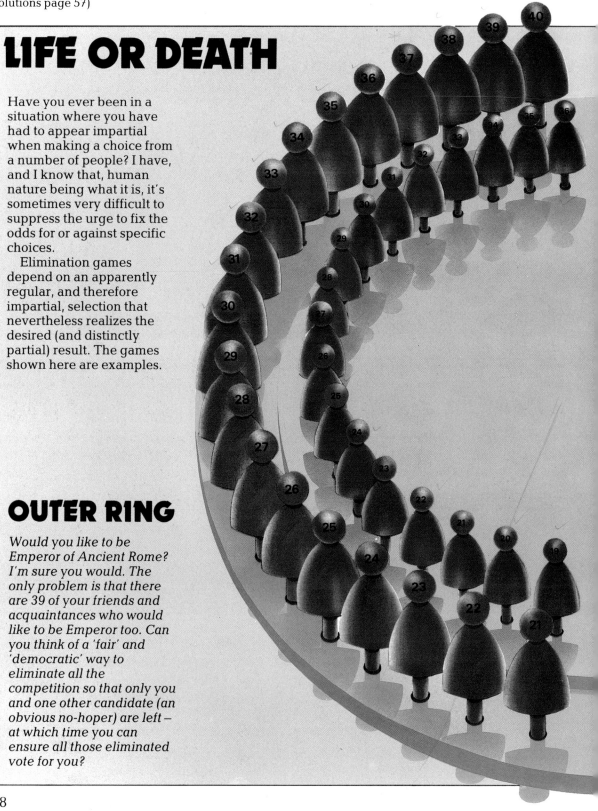

Arrange everyone as in the large outer ring on these two pages, and employ the 'old Roman custom' (which you've just invented) of selection by removing every third candidate (so number three is the first to go) and continuing as many times round the circle as necessary.

At which numbers in the circle should you and your chosen co-finalist stand to be sure that you both remain when everyone else has been eliminated?

INNER RING

Now you are Emperor, one of your first duties is to condemn 36 prisoners to be eaten by lions in the arena. The lions are roaring – but mostly because of stomach ache: the most they can eat today is 6 victims. Curiously, there are 6 among the prisoners who you'd prefer to go first . . . but how can you select them while seeming to remain impartial?

The (genuine) Roman custom of decimation gives you an idea: you arrange all 36 in a circle (as shown) and then pick out every tenth until you have the 6 the lions need. How do you do this to make sure that 'by chance' you pick the right 6?

(Solutions page 57)

FROM PILLAR TO POST

When I was young I used to play in a small enclosed courtyard that had eight pillars round the outside. In the middle was an octagonal flowerbed with a low surrounding fence. I played a game in which I tried to run from pillar to pillar for as long as possible without repeating my track. I could cross my previous tracks and even hop over the fence and run across the flowerbed if necessary (if my father wasn't looking). But there was one rule: if the only track left from one pillar to any other led down one side of the octagonal fence, the game ended.

This is an example of one attempt. I could travel to a pillar any number of times as long as each time it was from another direction and as long as I left again in a new direction. In this try, though, after my thirteenth move there was only a track down the side of the fence left and so I lost!

See how many moves you can make before you too are blocked. There are four outlines for you to play on.

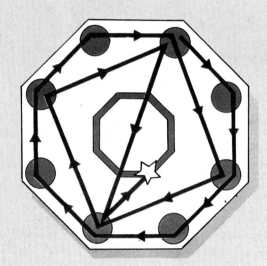

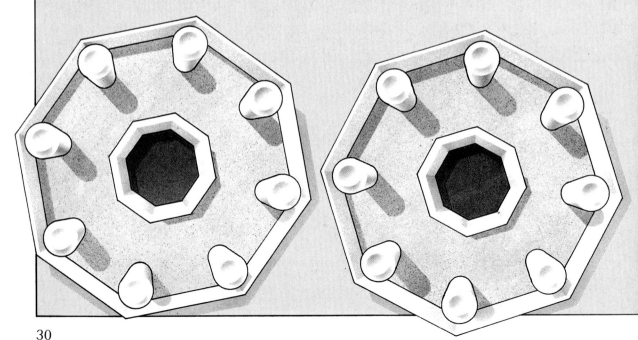

POSTING THE MAIL

At the center of a circular housing complex near where I live stands the communal mailbox – thirteen boxes on a central pillar. Two twins, known locally as Left and Right, deliver newspapers in the area, and they habitually play a game with the mailboxes. Each in turn slots a newspaper either into one mailbox only or into two adjacent mailboxes: the winner is the one who slots a newspaper into the last available box or boxes.

Using your left and right hands (and a pencil if you need to) and starting with your left, can you devise a strategy by which your right hand always wins the game?

(Solutions page 58)

GRIDLOCK

Getting across town by car can be a nightmare, not because of the traffic but because the crazy road signs always seem to force you to go where you don't want. In the town of Gridlock, the problem is even worse: the town traffic authorities have increased the number of signposts, and have invented some new ones, so that at most crossroads there is at least one way you cannot turn. Getting from one side of town to the other now involves some surprising twists and turns.

Can you find a route across town – beginning on the left and ending on the right – following the signs at the exit of every street at each junction?

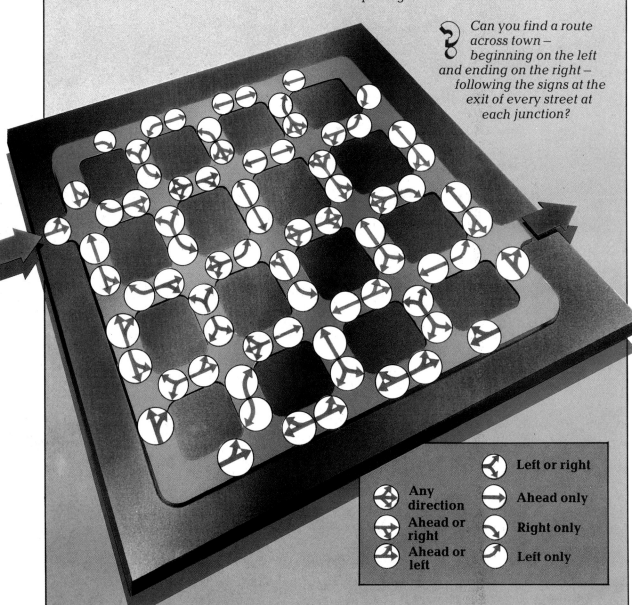

Any direction	Left or right
Ahead or right	Ahead only
Ahead or left	Right only
	Left only

CROSS ROADS

For this puzzle you need seven coins or counters. The challenge is to place all seven coins in sequence on seven of the eight circles.

But to do this every coin must first be placed on an empty circle and slid along one of the two associated lines to the circle where it will remain. The difficulty increases as you play: can you continue to find empty circles so you can follow the rules and move coins where you want them?

There is a simple strategy to complete the puzzle every time, no matter where you start. Can you work it out?

(Solutions page 58)

SEPARATE AND CONNECT

The common theme behind the puzzles on these two pages is that of combination, either in linking an expression or in creating groups from the constituents of a linear collection.

CUTTING THE NECKLACE

Imagine you are a pearl-fisher. Yesterday you dived and found only 6 pearls, which you put on a string, knowing that with just two cuts (as shown below) your partner, who makes up the pearl necklaces, could obtain any number of pearls up to all 6:

1 by itself
2 as a pair
3 as a trio
4 as 3 + 1
5 as 3 + 2
6 as 3 + 2 + 1

Today you have found 23. Where, in the string of 23, should you make four cuts in order to be able to obtain any number between 1 and 23?

FACTORIAL FORTY

There are four numbers between 1 and 40 (inclusive) that singly or in different combinations, with a plus or minus sign placed between them, can total *every* number between 1 and 40. No number occurs more than once in any expression.

What are they? Can you fill in the table below with combinations of these four?

	= 1		= 11		= 21		= 31
	= 2		= 12		= 22		= 32
	= 3		= 13		= 23		= 33
	= 4		= 14		= 24		= 34
	= 5		= 15		= 25		= 35
	= 6		= 16		= 26		= 36
	= 7		= 17		= 27		= 37
	= 8		= 18		= 28		= 38
	= 9		= 19		= 29		= 39
	= 10		= 20		= 30		= 40

The four numbers are:

MISSING LINKS

Below, in large figures, is an equation in which all the plus or minus signs have been left out. It is also possible that two of the numbers in the equation should have been printed together as a single number.

Can you sort out the line so that it reads correctly? Two smaller number sequences are included for you to use for practice.

1 2 3 4 5 6 7 8 9 = 100	1 2 3 4 5 6 7 8 9 = 100

(Solutions page 59)

THE TOWER OF BRAHMA

Many years ago, in India, I heard of a legend that a Hindu priest is steadily counting out the life span of the universe by moving the 64 disks that form the Tower of Brahma at a rate of 1 per second.

My game, involving 4 disks, will not take so long. It can be solved in only 15 moves. You need 4 disks of different sizes: make your own or use 4 coins. Stack them up with the largest at the bottom and the smallest at the top. Assign a second and a third place that can be used for stacking.

RULES

The object of the game is to reproduce the original stack in the third stacking-place, using the second as a temporary transfer stage. Move only one disk at a time, and never allow a disk to rest on top of a *smaller* disk. The blank columns opposite are provided so you can draw in the disks to play the game. Alternatively play out the game with coins or counters on the larger 'board' on the right.

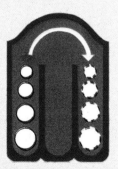

With 4 coins the transposition can be completed in 15 moves. How many moves does it take with only 3 coins?

36

THE LEGEND

An ancient Hindu holy man told me long ago that, in a certain great temple at Benares, there is a brass plate into which are fixed three pins. On one pin, at the beginning of time, there were 64 disks, the largest resting on the brass plate and the rest stacked up on top of it, in order of gradually decreasing size. Day and night, a priest transfers the disks from one pin to another at a rate of one per second, never allowing any disk to be placed on top of a smaller one, in order that one day the original Tower will be rebuilt, all 64 disks in sequence, on one of the other two pins. That day will be the end of the World. How much time do we have?

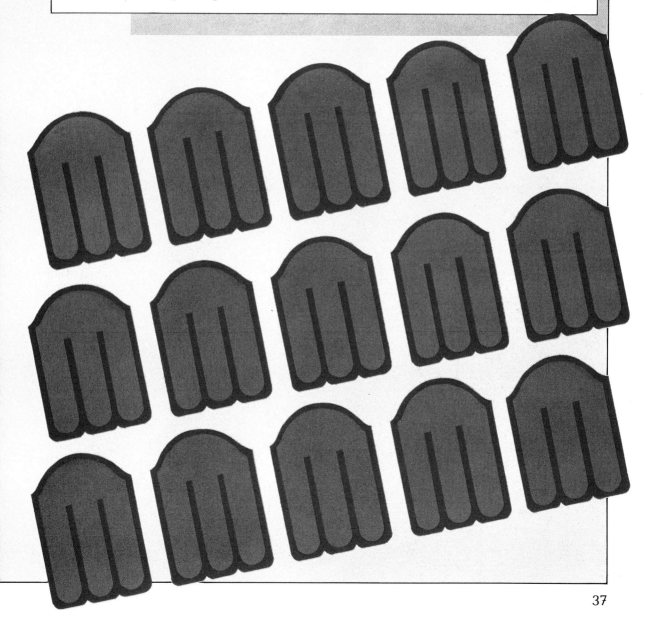

1 TE PLA ETA Y COU 1E

In my dream, I looked at the passengers and groaned. My job as Interplanetary Courier at the Alpha Centauri spaceport means that I am responsible for transporting passengers from the spaceport up to the spaceliner circling in planetary orbit many zerks above us. And what passengers! In front of me stand a Rigellian, a Denebian and a weird-looking quadripedal creature called a Terrestrial. The shuttle craft can carry only two 'people' at a time, and I am obliged to be one of them – but there are several nasty problems about that.

First, the Rigellians and the Denebians are officially at war: left together by themselves in the airlock one of these two will be certain to suffer an unfortunate 'accident'. Then, unlike the vegetarian Rigellian, the Denebian is voraciously carnivorous: left alone with the feeble Terrestrial for a second, there will very quickly be one fatter Denebian and no Terrestrial. Yet they all have to be ferried up to the liner's airlock, from which all three must pass into the care of the pretty reptilian hostesses.

It will take me a few trips and one passenger will have to accompany me more than once, but I can finally manage it. No one will have any accident; and no one will be eaten. And all three will emerge safely from the liner's airlock together.

How can I organize my trips? Do I need all the shuttle trips shown?

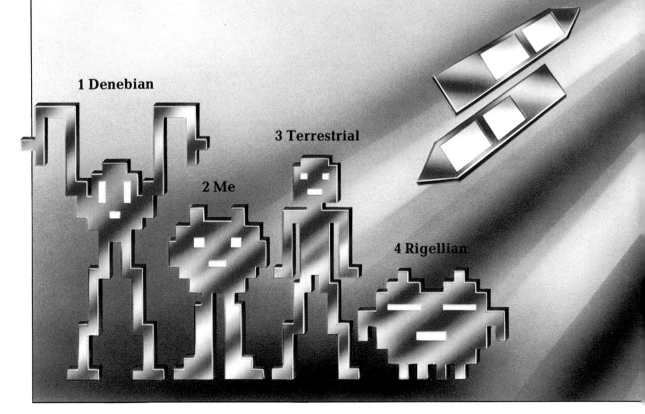

1 Denebian

3 Terrestrial

2 Me

4 Rigellian

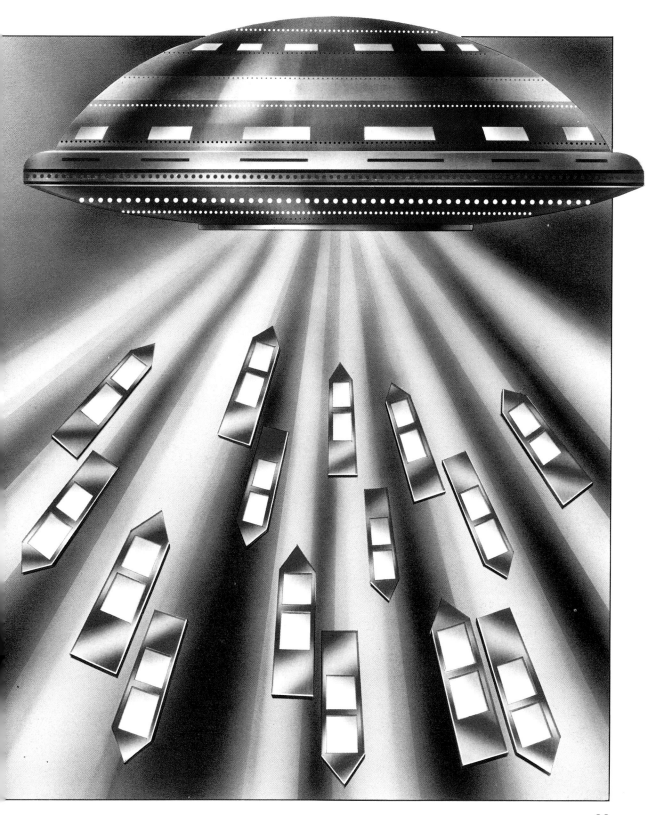

HUSBANDS AND WIVES

In days of long ago it was the convention that husbands would gallantly – and vigilantly – protect their vulnerable wives. So much so, that when three couples staying on an island together wanted to cross the surrounding water using a boat that could hold only two people at a time, a complicated scheme had first to be worked out to ensure that no wife was ever on the island or the mainland with a man who was not her own husband unless her husband was present too. She would be safe in the

START

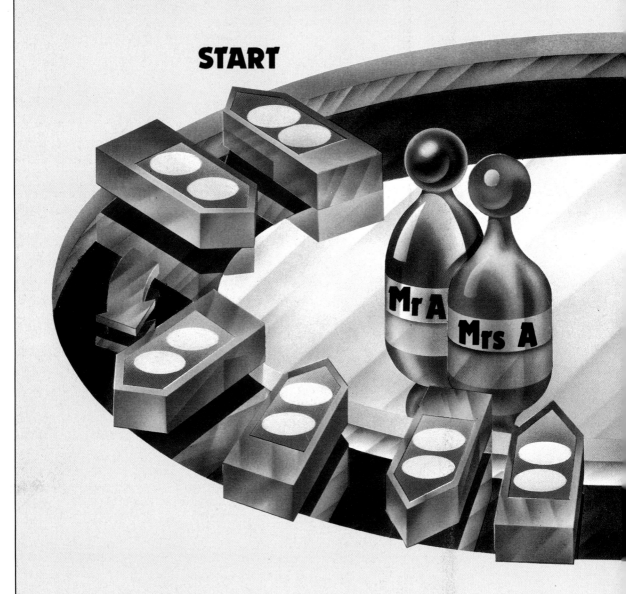

presence of other women, or alone.

In consequence the boat had to cross the water from or back to the island eleven times in all, before the three couples were united again as a complete group on the mainland.

Can you work out which passenger or passengers the boat had to carry on each of the eleven crossings? To make things easier, let's call the passengers Mr and Mrs A, Mr and Mrs B and Mr and Mrs C.

FINISH

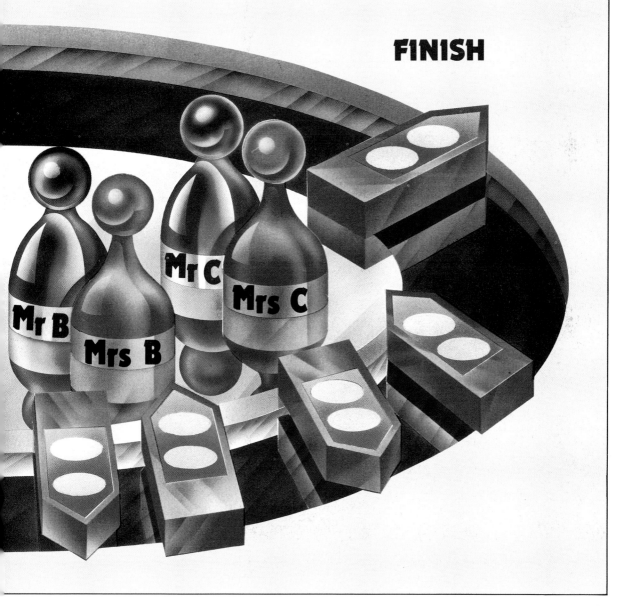

(Solutions page 61)

THE OCTOPUS HANDSHAKE

Down, deep down among the coral reefs, where the fish disport in the dim green depths, live two octopuses. They dwell in domestic bliss among the encrusted timbers of a sunken Spanish treasure ship. They have invented two games with nine 'pieces of eight' they have found. One is simple and one more difficult.

GAME 1

For the simple game, number the facets of each octagonal disk from 1 through 8 in such a way that the facets which meet the next disk do so at an identical number.

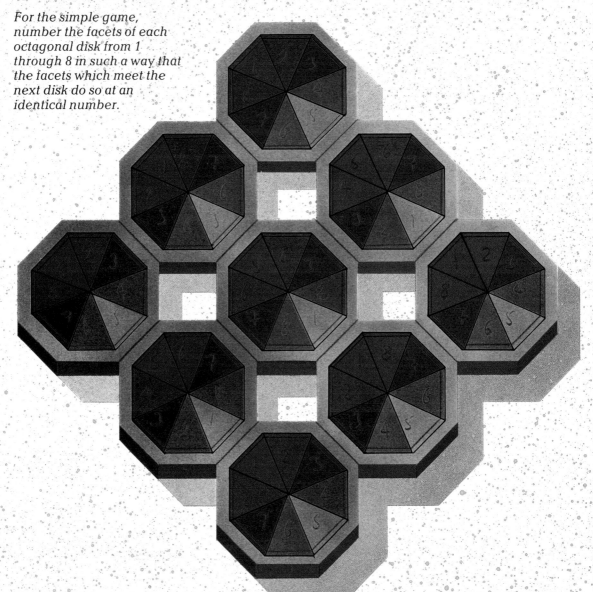

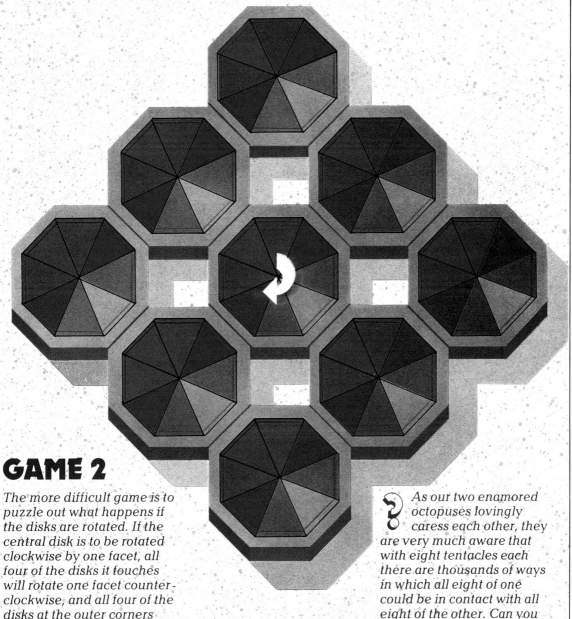

GAME 2

The more difficult game is to puzzle out what happens if the disks are rotated. If the central disk is to be rotated clockwise by one facet, all four of the disks it touches will rotate one facet counter-clockwise, and all four of the disks at the outer corners will rotate one facet clockwise (like the central disk).

Can you number the facets now so that after the rotation each facet which meets another disk will do so at an identical number?

And furthermore, if in Game 1 the facets touched at even numbers, can you make the rotated facets in this game touch at odd numbers? Or vice versa?

As our two enamored octopuses lovingly caress each other, they are very much aware that with eight tentacles each there are thousands of ways in which all eight of one could be in contact with all eight of the other. Can you calculate the total number of combinations, one-to-one, that are possible?

How many are possible if each tentacle of one octopus touches each of the other only once?

43

(Solutions page 61)

CALCULATING THE ODDS

Pascal's Triangle can be used for several different types of calculation related to probability, or calculating the odds.

Suppose, for example, you were offered any two of four objects. The possible number of different combinations of two may be found on the triangle by reading along row 4 (beginning 1, 4, 6 . . .) and noting that the second figure along (after the initial 1, which must be ignored) is 6. This shows that there are 6 possible combinations of any two of four.

If there is a chance element, the way to find out the chances of a specific two turning up from a total of four is to look at row 4 and compare the second along (6 again) with the total of all the numbers in the row. The result is a ratio of 6:16, or 3:8.

The pattern consists of an infinite arrangement of numbers in rows, each row having one more number than the one above it, and each internal number being the sum of the two numbers above it.

I have filled in the first few rows of the Pascal's Triangle for you. Can you complete the other rows as far as shown on this page?

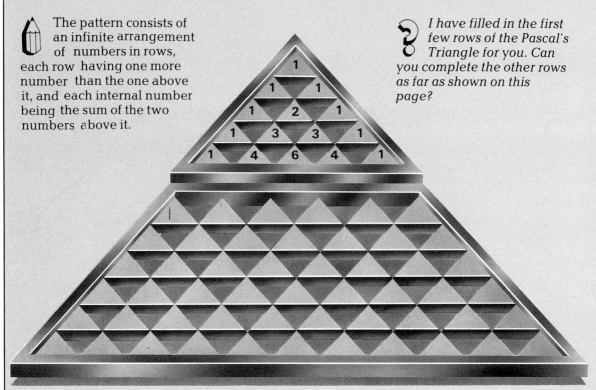

PASCAL'S TRIANGLE

Blaise Pascal was a French mathematician and philosopher; he was born in 1623. One of his many great contributions to math was his part in laying the foundations of probability theory, and it was during his research in this field that he made use of a special triangular pattern of numbers. The pattern can be traced back to the ancient Chinese – but is now generally called Pascal's Triangle because of the ingenious applications he found for it.

DICEY PROBLEMS

On this page there are two representations of the possible combinations resulting from throwing two dice.

One is a form of chart, showing the numerical totals made by combining the dice at the top and side of the grid.

The other shows the dice-faces that go to make up those numerical totals, from 2 through 12.

Because the possible total 7 can result from 6 different combinations out of 36, we say that that total has a 6:36 – or 1:6 – chance of occurring. Likewise the totals 2 and 12 have only a 1:36 chance of occurring.

How many combinations are there which have a 1:9 chance of occurring? How many combinations are there which have a 1:12 chance of occurring? And what totals do they involve?

This is not quite as easy as you might think at first.

Both prove that there are 36 possible combinations. Both also show that the combinations totaling 2 and 12 occur only once each among the possible 36 – and the chances of throwing either are therefore 1:36. Finally, both also prove that the total 7 is the most common result, occurring six times in 36 – and the chances of throwing such a combination is thus 6:36 or 1:6.

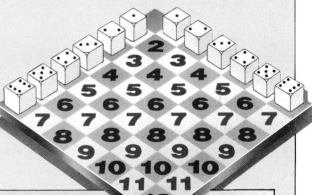

GAUSSIAN CURVE

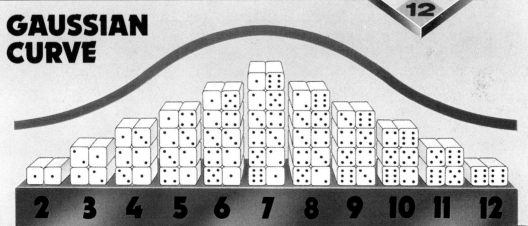

All the possible combinations of two dice are shown in dice-faces, resulting in totals between 2 and 12. The columns in turn represent the 'normal' or Gaussian curve – a graph that is fundamental to probability theory.

45

(Solutions page 62)

UP IN THE AIR

If you're a gambler, you'll know that when you calculate odds it is very important that you know the exact number of different possible outcomes. It is also valuable to know about any ways in which those outcomes can be usefully predicted.

The puzzle on these pages explores all the possible outcomes if five small colored balls are tossed into five tubs. Every ball lands in a tub, but some may land in the same tub – there is room enough for all five to do so – and some tubs may therefore remain empty.

Once you have found out all the possible combinations of balls in tubs – from a single ball in each tub to all five in one tub – you can get down to thinking about mathematical probabilities.

On these two pages there are 58 groups of five tubs. Try to work out all the possible distributions of the five balls that drop into them. It is fairly evident that there can be only one way of distributing all five balls in one tub; there is also only one way to put all five balls each in a separate tub – but what are the chances of either happening? You will need to know the total number of possibilities.

Use colored pencils to draw in the balls, or use numbers or letters to represent the different balls. (This shows that the puzzle can be solved mathematically too.)

Hint You will not need *all* of the tubs on these pages.

 What are the odds that the five balls will fall into three tubs? Or that they will drop in a four-plus-one formation?

46

(Solutions page 63)

LUCKY SPINNER, LUCKY DICE

Here's some mathematical logic to do with 'transitivity'. If object A is bigger than object B, which is bigger than object C, it follows that A must be bigger than C. Certain games appear to disobey this principle – and are thus said to exhibit 'nontransitivity'.

One type of game, for example, like the children's game of scissors, paper and stone, has a circular winning arrangement: scissors cut paper, paper wraps stone, and stone blunts scissors. If two players play such a game it is possible for one to be very lucky and win every time – the odds are not even. This ceases to be the case, however, if three play.

The games on these two pages are based on what happens when three do play this sort of game, and on the bias inherent in an apparently random chance of results.

GAME 1

The first game uses three spinners, which point to a value after being spun. The first spinner (A) has only one value: 3. The second spinner (B) is more complex; just over half of it (56%) has a value of 2, and just under half (the remaining 44%) is equally divided between values of 4 and 6. The third spinner (C) is divided so that fractionally over half of it (51%) is worth 1 and the rest is worth 5. The game involves spinning the arrows to see which spinner beats which.

48

C

5

1

Which is the most successful spinner if there is to be a series of spins?

Is it going to be any less successful, do you think, if there is to be only one spin of each spinner?

Can you prove your answer mathematically either way?

GAME 2

Here we have a special set of four dice. Just how special it is can be seen from the 'plans' of the six faces of each of them – A, B, C and D. The set is carefully designed to demonstrate non-transitivity.

Looking at the numbers on each dice, can you see why A beats B, B beats C, C beats D, and D beats A – and what is the probability involved?

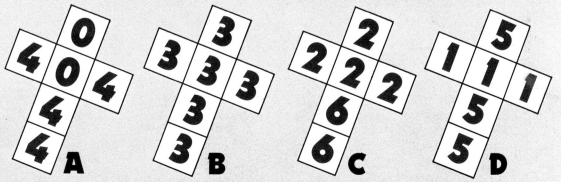

49

TH- JOLUTION

MATCH BLOCKS PAGE 8-9

There are several possible solutions to both games. The ones presented here are among the most obvious.

Game 1

7	6	5	4	3	2	1
1	7	6	5	4	3	2
2	1	7	6	5	4	3
3	2	1	7	6	5	4
4	3	2	1	7	6	5
5	4	3	2	1	7	6
6	5	4	3	2	1	7

Game 2

7	5	3	1	6	4	2
1	6	4	2	7	5	3
2	7	5	3	1	6	4
3	1	6	4	2	7	5
4	2	7	5	3	1	6
5	3	1	6	4	2	7
6	4	2	7	5	3	1

MATCH BLOCKS

Match blocks in these same combinations can also be arranged to form a Magic Square (see p. 16), in which all rows, columns and diagonals add up to the same number. In fact, the solutions to these puzzles set fulfil all the requirements of Magic Squares – inevitably so, because the numbers 1 through 7 are being arranged specifically to fall in each direction only once. The number each row/column/diagonal adds up to is thus the total sum of the numbers 1 through 7 . . . which is 28. These match block puzzles were inspired by a special category of Magic Squares discovered by the Swiss mathematician Leonhard Euler and named by him Latin Squares.

FINDING THE KEY PAGE 10-11

KEY TO THE KEYS

If you change only one shape, you will need to alter three key tops, and arrange these so that two are separated from the third by one original shape, so that you can identify both the starting point (one different top) and the direction (two different tops together) in which to count the memorized sequence.

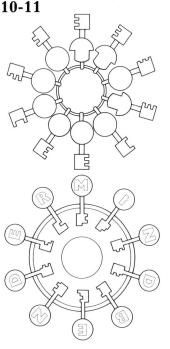

COMBINATION LOCK

There are three repeated letters to be found. The secret code word is:
M I N D B E N D E R

FINDING THE KEY

Key to the Keys
As with several other problems in this book, this puzzle is most easily solved by choosing a place on the circle to start at, and by considering the keys to form a straight line from there. In other words, the puzzle can be simplified by looking at it in linear – as opposed to circular – terms. This is an important principle, although in all of such cases it is also essential to remember that one end of your 'line' is in fact contiguous with the other.

CONTINUOUS PATHS PAGE 12-13

The starting node for the sample game and Game A is the only one possible – because all arrows lead away from it so unless you start there, that node will never be reached.

Similarly, there is only one node from which Game B can start. Game B can end only at the node shown, because all arrows point to it and none points away.

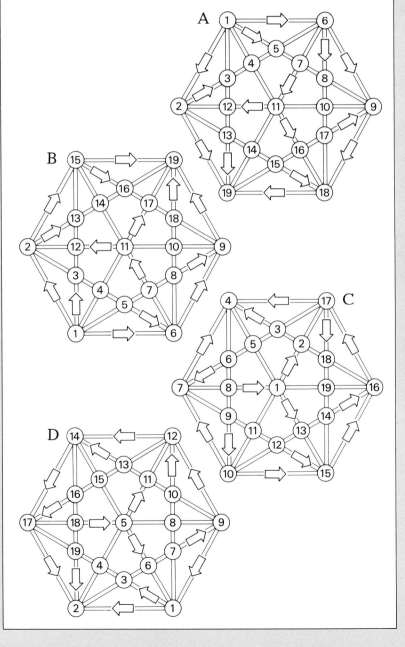

CONTINUOUS PATHS

This puzzle is based on a far more complex version first presented as a problem for scientists to work out mathematically by Sir William Rowan Hamilton in 1857. An Irishman, Hamilton was born in Dublin in 1805. He was very quickly renowned as a prodigy, being able to read English at the age of three, Latin, Greek and Hebrew by the age of five, and Arabic and Sanskrit by the time he was ten. Two years later he read Isaac Newton's <u>Arithmetica Universalis</u> – and was hooked on math for the rest of his life. In 1822 he found an error in the work of the eminent French mathematician-astronomer Pierre-Simon Laplace (whose major and authoritative <u>Celestial Mechanics</u> was in the process of publication by instalments), and made it known to the Irish Royal Astronomer. The consequence was that after a brilliant episode studying at Trinity College, Dublin, Hamilton himself became Irish Royal Astronomer at the age of 22. Math remained his first love, however, and particularly number theory and forms of calculus.

It was in relation to what he called Icosian calculus that he began devising path-tracing problems on solid figures, to be solved mathematically. Aren't you glad I haven't asked you to do that?

SLIDING COINS PAGE 14-15

Shown move by move, the best answers I can achieve in each game are illustrated below.

Game 1

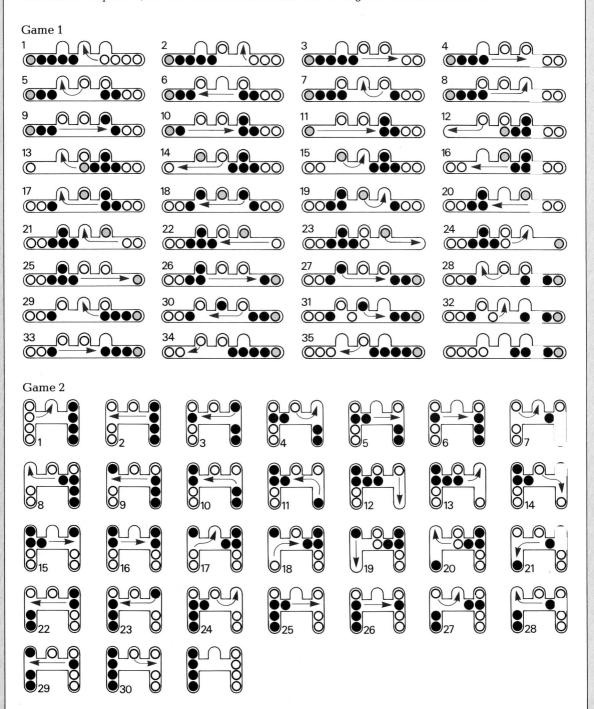

Game 2

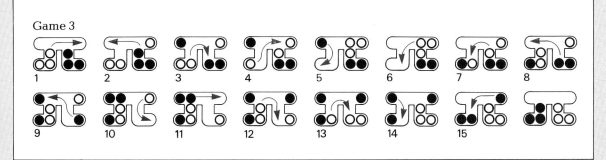

Game 3

1 2 3 4 5 6 7 8

9 10 11 12 13 14 15

MAGIC NUMBERS PAGE 16-17

The Magic Cross, Wheel and Hexagon have many solutions of which these are examples.

Magic Cross   Magic Wheel   Magic Hexagon

THE SIX-POINT STAR
Using the Magic Number 26, there are 80 possible solutions. This is one.

To find an optimal total for a Magic Star's Magic Number, add all the numbers to be distributed, double that, and divide by the number of points of the Star.

A quicker method – which usually works – is to double the highest number and add two.

Note: It is impossible to complete a Five-point Star.

THE SEVEN-POINT STAR
Using the Magic Number 30, there are 56 possible solutions. This is one.

THE EIGHT-POINT STAR
Using the Magic Number 34, there are 112 possible solutions. This is one.

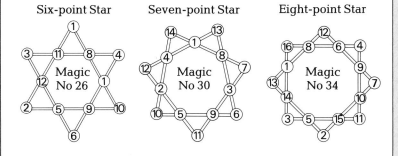

Six-point Star
Magic No 26

Seven-point Star
Magic No 30

Eight-point Star
Magic No 34

MAGIC NUMBERS (1) AND (2)

The 3 × 3 Magic Square in which the numbers 1 through 9 were distributed is the earliest known of this type of problem, and has been traced back as far as fourth-century BC China. To the ancient Chinese, this *Lo-shu* represented either the universe or China, and its middle number therefore represented either the center of the universe or the Emperor – in Chinese eyes these were effectively the same thing. Chinese mathematicians went on to construct 5 × 5 and 7 × 7 Magic Squares of various types, although they found it a little more difficult with 4 × 4 and 6 × 6 Squares and eventually came to regard these as ominous.

It was for its 'lucky' properties that the 3 × 3 Magic Square became popular in the Arab world in the tenth century AD. The associations of such Squares with the universe, introduced contemporaneously, quickly lent them religious interpretations, as expounded in an encyclopedia published in about 989 by the Brotherhood of Purity. Sufi mystics saw the Squares as representations of Life in constant motion, renewed and rejuvenated by the source of power at the heart of the universal design.

The Hindus of medieval India regarded 4 × 4 and 6 × 6 Magic Squares as particularly potent and lucky, and went on to construct larger Squares of even-numbered sides, eventually establishing a sophisticated methodology for doing so.

MAGIC NUMBERS 2 PAGE 18-19

Examples of answers to the Magic Square puzzles are shown below. There is always more than one possible answer because most puzzles remain equally valid if rows are reversed horizontally or vertically.

4 × 4 Magic Squares

3 × 3 Magic Squares

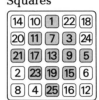

5 × 5 Magic Squares

Magic Squares finally permeated Western consciousness in the sixteenth century through links with Islamic countries and Hebrew interpretations in Cabalistic texts. Two centuries later, the great Swiss mathematician Leonhard Euler was fascinated by them, as was his contemporary Benjamin Franklin, who invented a type all of his own.

COMBI-CARDS PAGE 20-21

The sets of Combi-cards should be divided and numbered as shown below.

Four cards

1	1	2	3
2	4	4	5
3	5	6	6

Five cards

1	1	2	3	4
2	5	5	6	7
3	6	8	8	9
4	7	9	10	10

Six cards

1	1	2	3	4	5
2	6	6	7	8	9
3	7	10	10	11	12
4	8	11	13	13	14
5	9	12	14	15	15

The highest numbers of these three series are 6, 10 and 15, representing a mathematical progression of

$$\frac{4 \times 3}{2} \ (=6) \qquad \frac{5 \times 4}{2} \ (=10) \qquad \frac{6 \times 5}{2} \ (=15)$$

so that the highest number on a seven-card set will be

$$\frac{7 \times 6}{2} \text{ or } 21$$

COMBI-CARDS

There is good reasoning behind the mathematical equations given as part of the answers above. The highest number in each set represents:

the number of cards × the number of numbers on each card
————————————————————
the number of times each number is included (always 2)

An interestingly varied set of cards is obtained if each number on the cards is allocated a different color. For those of you who have an aversion to figures a set of colored cards may prove a more enjoyable challenge.

MONEY PROBLEMS PAGE 22-23

A RING OF COINS
Shown below is the quickest
way of completing the ring.

GAME 1 COIN SOLITAIRE
Shown here are the five moves
that leave only one coin. It
makes little difference which
space is left free at the
beginning.

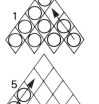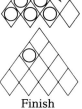

Finish

COIN SOLITAIRE GAME 2
Shown here are our nine moves to complete the game.

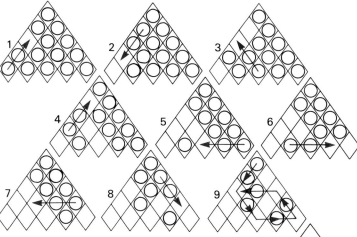

The space left free at the beginning must
be the center one of any outside row of five;
spaces 4, 6 or 13. These spaces are
topologically equivalent, as the shape is an
equilateral triangle.

Finish

MONEY PROBLEMS

Games 2 and 3
This kind of solitaire is in essence a
means of playing checkers by
oneself. It is interesting to note,
though, that the first recorded use of
the word 'solitaire' in English in
reference to this game – more often
called pegboard solitaire now, in
order to distinguish it from the
solitaire card games – occurred ten
years before the publication of the
first authoritative study of checkers,
William Payne's *Guide to the Game
of Draughts* (with a dedication
written by Dr Samuel Johnson) in
1756. It is also debatable whether, in
reference to this game, it is the
player who is meant to be 'solitary'
(the meaning of *solitaire* in French)
or the single coin left at the end of a
successful game.

THE 18-POINT PROBLEM PAGE 24-25

The eleventh level problem can be solved as shown below.

The 18-point problem is explained, see right.

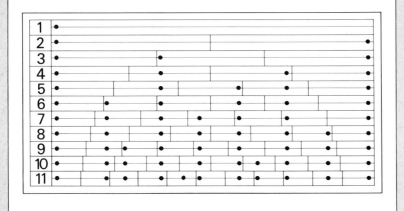

THE 18-POINT PROBLEM

It has been suggested, fairly authoritatively, that – even with the utmost foresight – the seventeenth dot is the farthest that anyone can ordinarily get. Well, I gave you a chance to get to the eighteenth, anyway. Maybe it takes a microscope to be able to go farther still.

The real reason is, however, that by that stage the vertical lines are clustering so thickly, each space between them 'moving' either toward the center or toward the outsides, that any specific space has in fact traveled right across previous borders *and into the next.*

JUMPING COINS PAGE 26-27

GAME 1
With six counters, the solution can be reached in 15 moves. See right.

GAME 2
With eight counters, the solution can be reached in 24 moves. See below.

GAME 3
With ten counters, the solution can be reached in 35 moves. See FORMULA.

Game 1

Game 2

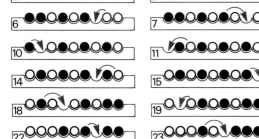

JUMPING COINS – FORMULA

This game is illustrated move by move for Games 1 and 2. These moves can be summarized by a 'formula' as shown here. In Game 1, using six counters, the sequence starts with one move by either of the center counters into the middle space. It is then followed by two moves by counters of the other type, then three moves from the first type, and so on alternately for three moves, then two moves, then one move. The total number of moves for each game can be calculated by adding the sequence shown. Mathematically, the minimum number of moves can be seen as: y (half the number of counters) × (y + 2). Thus Game 1: $3 \times 5 = 15$ Game 2: $4 \times 6 = 24$ Game 3: $5 \times 7 = 35$.

Game 1

1+2+3+3+3+2+1 = 15

Game 2

1+2+3+4+4+4+3+2+1 = 24

Game 3

1+2+3+4+5+5+5+4+3+2+1 = 35

LIFE OR DEATH PAGE 28-29

Congratulations on becoming Emperor of Rome! It was brilliant of you and your proposed co-candidate to take up positions 13 and 28 in the circle of 40.

If you have arranged things correctly, the lion's lunch should have been numbers 4, 10, 15, 20, 26 and 30 in the original circle of 36.

The mathematical formula for solving such problems has eluded mathematicians for centuries. Practical solutions are best achieved by trial and error.

FROM PILLAR TO POST PAGE 30-31

The theoretical maximum number of lines I could have run along is 20. No matter how many different ways I tried to run, I could never get beyond 17. If the courtyard had had seven or even nine pillars, however, the full complement would have been easier to achieve. I realized that for reasons of topology the full complement of 20 continuous tracks is impossible. The general rule is that if there are more than two nodes from which an odd number of lines emerge, the network cannot be completed with a continuous line . . . and all eight nodes of the courtyard have potentially five lines emerging from them.

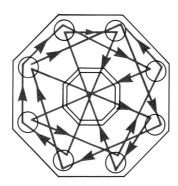

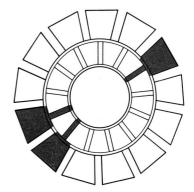

POSTING THE MAIL

The strategy by which the right hand can always win is simple to follow. If the left hand starts with one newspaper in one mailbox, the right hand puts two in the two mailboxes opposite. If the left hand starts with two papers in two boxes, the right then puts just one in the opposite box. (Because there are 13 boxes, one box can be opposite two, and vice versa.) Either way, after this opening response, the right hand merely repeats whatever the left hand does, and always gets the last move.

GRIDLOCK PAGE 32

You can cross town like this:

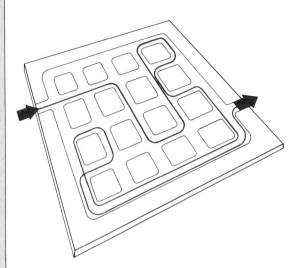

CROSSROADS PAGE 33

Remember that each time you place a coin on a circle to move to a successive one, that circle is to be the final destination of the next coin. There will always be one pathway free, using this strategy.

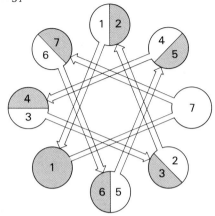

SEPARATE AND CONNECT PAGE 34-35

CUTTING THE NECKLACE

Make your cuts each side of the fourth pearl and each side of the eleventh pearl; then you have the sequence: 1 to 3, 4, 5 to 10, 11, 12 to 23; which represents lengths of: 3 pearls, 1 pearl, 6 pearls, 1 pearl, 12 pearls; from whch it is possible to make up any number between 1 and 23.

FACTORIAL FORTY

The numbers are 1 3 9 27,

1	=1	9+3−1	=11	27−9+3	=21	27+3+1	=31
3−1	=2	9+3	=12	27−9+3+1	=22	27+9−3−1	=32
3	=3	9+3+1	=13	27−3−1	=23	27+9−3	=33
3+1	=4	27−9−3−1	=14	27−3	=24	27+9−3+1	=34
9−3−1	=5	27−9−3	=15	27−3+1	=25	27+9−1	=35
9−3	=6	27−9−3+1	=16	27−1	=26	27+9	=36
9−3+1	=7	27−9−1	=17	27	=27	27+9+1	=37
9−1	=8	27−9	=18	27+1	=28	27+9+3−1	=38
9	=9	27−9+1	=19	27+3−1	=29	27+9+3	=39
9+1	=10	27−9+3−1	=20	27+3	=30	27+9+3+1	=40

MISSING LINKS

$1 + 2 + 3 - 4 + 5 + 6 + 78 + 9 = 100$

SEPARATE AND CONNECT

Missing Links

A line of figures 1 through 9 followed by another figure which ends in a zero reminds us immediately of how securely our numeric system is based on the number ten. Although the decimal system now seems entirely familiar to us, other systems in other times have been based on other numbers. Historical evidence that the decimal system once meant far less than it does today may be observed in the way we measure time (in 60s or 12s), define angles (in 60s, basically) or even sell eggs (in 12s); even one's life span is said to be measured as though carving notches on a tally-stick – 'three *score* years and ten', following the practice of notching up a score for every twenty.

By the way, if in my introduction to this puzzle I had said it was possible that *three* of the numbers in the equation should have been printed as a single number, your answer could have been:
$123 - 4 - 5 - 6 - 7 + 8 - 9 = 100$
just as if I had not limited the symbols to be inserted to plus or minus signs, another solution could have been:
$12 + 34 + (5 \times 6) + 7 + 8 + 9 = 100$

TOWER OF BRAHMA PAGE 36–37

With four counters it takes 15 moves as shown below.

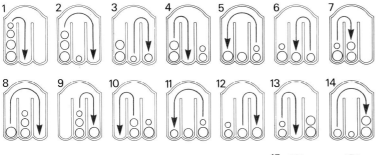

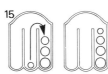

With three counters it takes seven moves.
With five counters it would take 31 moves.
With 64 counters it would take more or less forever.

THE TOWER OF BRAHMA

Let's be more precise. With 64 disks the number of moves necessary to move the tower is 18,446,744,073,709,551,615. And at one per second, that would take around 585,000 million years – not actually for ever, perhaps, but more than a hundred times the duration of the universe as presently calculated.

The formula for calculating the numbers of moves required is $2^n - 1$, where n = the numbers of disks. For 3 disks, this gives $2^3 - 1 = 7$; for 4 disks, $2^4 - 1 = 15$; for 5 disks, $2^5 - 1 = 31$; and for 64 disks, $2^{64} - 1$, which is the number given above.

INTERPLANETARY COURIER PAGE 38–39

This is how my trips can be organized. It takes only seven trips.

All four of us begin at the spaceport:

Rigellian
Denebian
Terrestrial
Me

---

1. I take the Denebian up to the liner:

Rigellian	Denebian
Terrestrial	Me

---

2. I return alone:

Rigellian	Denebian
Terrestrial	
Me	

---

3. I take the Rigellian up to the liner:

Terrestrial	Rigellian
	Denebian
	Me

---

4. I return with the Denebian:

Denebian	
Terrestrial	Rigellian
Me	

---

5. I take the Terrestrial up to the liner:

Denebian	Rigellian
	Terrestrial
	Me

---

6. I return alone:

Denebian	Rigellian
Me	Terrestrial

---

7. I take the Denebian up to the liner:

	Rigellian
	Denebian
	Terrestrial
	Me

And we all go through the airlock, into the tender care of the hostesses.

HUSBANDS AND WIVES PAGE 40–41

CROSSINGS	ISLAND	MAINLAND
initial situation	Mr A. Mrs A. Mr B. Mrs B. Mr C. Mrs C.	
first crossing to mainland – Mr A. Mrs A.	Mr B. Mrs B. Mr C. Mrs C.	Mr A. Mrs A.
second crossing to island – Mr A.	Mr A. Mr B. Mrs B. Mr C. Mrs C.	Mrs A.
third crossing to mainland – Mrs B. Mrs C.	Mr A. Mr B. Mr C.	Mrs A. Mrs B. Mrs C.
fourth crossing to island – Mrs A.	Mr A. Mrs A Mr B. Mr C.	Mrs B. Mrs C.
fifth crossing to mainland – Mr B. Mr C.	Mr A. Mrs A.	Mr B. Mrs B. Mr C. Mrs C.
sixth crossing to island – Mr B. Mrs B.	Mr A. Mrs A. Mr B. Mrs B.	Mr C. Mrs C.
seventh crossing to mainland – Mr A. Mr B.	Mrs A. Mrs B.	Mr A. Mr B. Mr C. Mrs C.
eighth crossing to island – Mrs C.	Mrs A. Mrs B. Mrs C.	Mr A. Mr B. Mr C.
ninth crossing to mainland – Mrs B. Mrs C.	Mrs A.	Mr A. Mr B. Mrs B. Mr C. Mrs C.
tenth crossing to island – Mr A.	Mr A. Mrs A.	Mr B. Mrs B. Mr C. Mrs C.
eleventh crossing to mainland – Mr A. Mrs A.		Mr A. Mrs A. Mr B. Mrs B. Mr C. Mrs C.

HUSBANDS AND WIVES

This is just one of many such problems relating to couples who are presented as inseparable in some way. Similar puzzles involving more than three couples require a boat that will hold more than two people at a time, however. For four or five couples, a boat that will take three people at a time is a necessity; and for six or more couples a four-seater boat is essential if the rules of inseparability as laid down here are to be followed.

THE OCTOPUS HANDSHAKE PAGE 42–43

The disks meet at even numbers, then odd numbers, as shown below. When rotated, they meet at identical numbers.

Game 1

Game 2

Our octopuses have experimented many times to find the most convenient way to work through all the possible combinations of eight tentacle contact. They finally struck on what is probably the easiest method: one of them stays still, tentacles outstretched and unmoving; the other then methodically works through every combination possible. This can be calculated by the following multiplication, known as

factorial 8: $1 \times 2 \times 3 \times 4 \times 5 \times 6 \times 7 \times 8$ which comes to 40,320 altogether. At 12 moves a minute it comes to 56 hours nonstop! There is no need for the static octopus to go through the whole routine as well – all the possible combinations have been done.

On the other tentacle, if no tentacle is to touch another more than once, the total possible combinations is reduced to 8×8, which is 64.

CALCULATING THE ODDS PAGE 44-45

PASCAL'S TRIANGLE

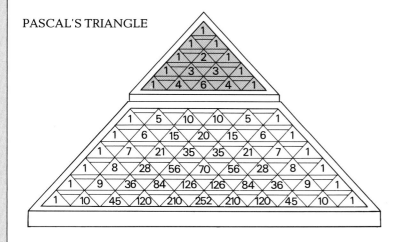

DICEY PROBLEMS
There are *eight* combinations which have a chance of 1:9 of occurring – not four. This is because combinations totaling 5 and those totaling 9 all have the same 1:9 chance of occurring, and there are four of each.

Likewise, there are *six* combinations which have a chance of 1:12 of occurring – not three. Combinations totaling 4 and 10 all have the same 1:12 chance of occurring, and there are three of each.

UP IN THE AIR PAGE 46-47

There are 52 possible outcomes, so the odds that all five will drop either into separate tubs or together all into one tub are both 1:52. If you carried the process out in practice once a week, this outcome would result on average once a year.

The odds on the five balls falling into three tubs are 25:52, or almost 1:2. This is made up from the fact that there are 10 possible outcomes of balls in a 1 + 1 + 3 formation, and 15 of balls in a 2 + 2 + 1 formation – a total of 25 landing in three tubs.

In a 4 + 1 formation there are only five possibilities (shown mathematically as: 1 + 2345, 2 + 1345, 3 + 1245, 4 + 1235, 5 + 1234) so the odds are 5:52, or between 1:10 and 1:11.

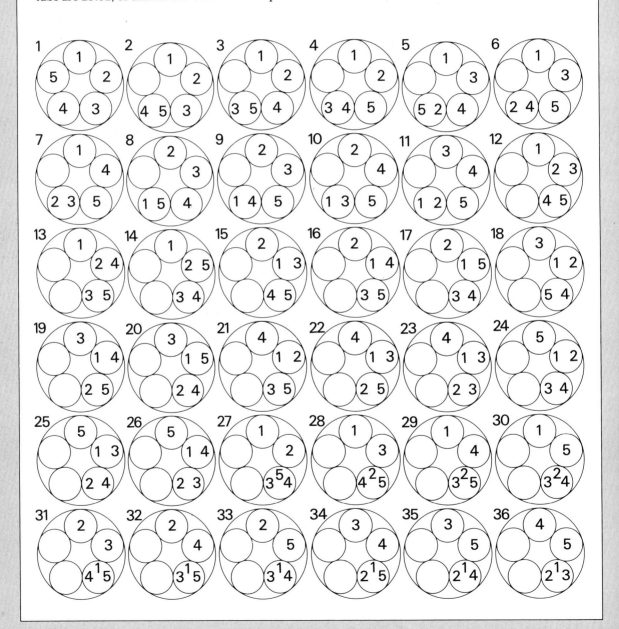

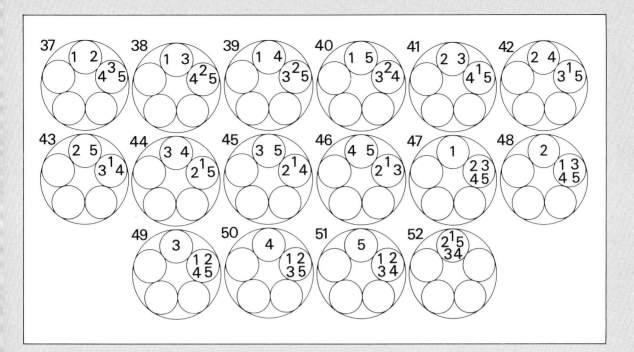

LUCKY SPINNERS, LUCKY DICE PAGE 48-49

LUCKY SPINNERS

In a series of spins, with each spinner matched against one other, spinner A is the most successful.

Out of 100 spins between A and B, spinner A beats spinner B, 56 times. This is because value 2 occupies 56% of the area of spinner B and so whenever the pointer of spinner B registers 2, spinner A, with value 3, wins. In terms of probability this is referred to as 0.56 probability. (Probability of 1 is certainty; of 0 is the opposite.)

Similarly, spinner A also beats spinner C, but only 51 times out of 100 as 51% of spinner C has a value less than spinner A. The probability in this case is 0.51.

If all spinners compete simultaneously, however, the chances of spinner A winning are dramatically reduced; in fact it is the worst choice. This is because the separate probabilities of spinner A beating the others must be combined, and $0.56 \times 0.51 = 0.28$, which means that out of 100 spins, spinner A would only win 28 times.

LUCKY DICE

When two six-sided dice are thrown together, there are 36 possible outcomes, as we saw on pages 44-45 (DICEY PROBLEMS). Taking dice A and B, therefore, we can see that 24 times out of 36, A will show value 4, therefore beating the value 3 of B (which appears 36 times). With B and C, value 2 of C appears 24 times, allowing B to win. With C and D, the answer is also 24. The fact that C beats D is shown in diagramatic form in the table below. A similar table can be completed to show that D beats A 24 out of 36 times too.

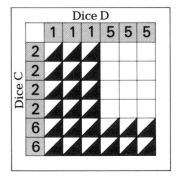

ACKNOWLEDGEMENTS

Eddison/Sadd Editions would like to acknowledge the assistance and cooperation received from Clark Robinson Limited during the production of this book.

Creative Director: Nick Eddison
Art Director: Gill Della Casa
Designer: Amanda Barlow

Editorial Director: Ian Jackson
Project Editor: Hal Robinson
Copywriter: Michael Darton
Proofreader: Christine Moffat

Artists:
Keith Duran (represented by Linden Artists) 18-19, 24-25, 40-41
Andrew Farmer 22-23, 28-29, 32-33, 34-35
Mick Gillah 8-9, 10-11, 12-13, 30-31, 46-47
Kuo Kang Chen 6-7, 38-39, 44-45, 48-49
Andy Pearson (represented by Ian Fleming & Associates Ltd) 20-21
Larry Rostant (represented by Artists Partners) 14-15, 16-17, 26-27, 36-37, 42-43
Solutions artwork:
Anthony Duke and Dave Sexton 50-63

THE FINAL SOLUTION – COVER PUZZLE

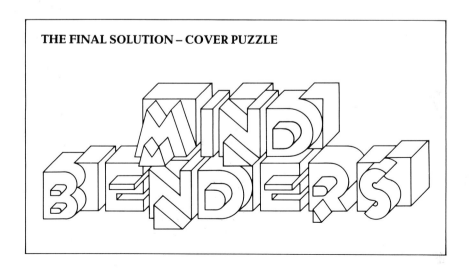